Yehudi Wyner

FANTASIES FOR PIANO

AMP 8177

First Printing: September 2002

ISBN 0-6340-4611-X

Associated Music Publishers, Inc.

DISTRIBUTED BY

HAL•LEONARD®
CORPORATION
7777 W. BLUEMOUND RD. P.O. BOX 13819 MILWAUKEE, WI 53213

THREE SHORT FANTASIES

NEW FANTASIES

POST FANTASIES

duration ca. 43'

A compact disc recording of THREE SHORT FANTASIES
is available from CRI: CD 701, Robert Miller piano

Composer's Note

Three Short Fantasies

The composition of *Three Short Fantasies* spans eight years. The first, fluently sketched in 1963, was evoked by the mysterious sonority of Stravinsky's *Symphonies for Wind Instruments*. For a number of years I set aside this Fantasy, unsure of its value (repelled, attracted, indifferent) until at last it persuaded me. I dedicated it to friends, P and B, under the title *Piccole Armonie*.

The second, subtitled *Piccola Fantasia Davenniana*, written during the summer of 1966, was a birthday present for the pianist Ward Davenny. The pitch structure derives from a simple system based on his name.

Short Fantasy 3 was completed expressly for Robert Miller to play in 1971, and is dedicated to him. His interest in the first two pieces and his unruffled confidence that the new piece would be ready in time for a recital at Lincoln Center helped turn long speculation into reality.

I feel the three fantasies live well together despite the years that separate them, despite the absence of a unifying idea or systematic program. Like the unplanned elements in a city, the pieces comprise a neighborhood. I say these things because I am interested in unity I cannot explain. Demonstrable unities and methodical construction often bore me with their simple-minded ingenuities, substituting "reasons" for the mystery of intuitive coherence.

New Fantasies

The *New Fantasies* (1991) are shards from the kiln, so to speak. While at the American Academy in Rome as Composer-in-Residence for the spring of 1991, I was completing a piece for the Boston Symphony Chamber Players and another for DaCapo, the New York based chamber ensemble. The inexorable deadlines seemed to be approaching with increasing speed and I needed to work with total concentration. Outside diversions were few, but inner digressions proliferated. Some grew directly out of the main work I was doing, a close examination of a chord progression, a series, a sonority. Other materials were altogether unrelated, unwelcome intruders on what I thought needed to be an exclusively focused context. If the unbidden visitors chose to stay, indeed obsessed me with their annoying insistence, I had no choice but to acknowledge them, taste and better judgement notwithstanding, and to listen to what they had to say. At a certain stage in our work the suspension of judgement may be the most important strategy we can embrace in order to liberate the unsuspected layers of our creative thought.

Dalla Cappella al Casino (from the Chapel to the Casino). My studio at the Academy was the former chapel of the Villa Aurelia, a palazzo of the Seventeenth Century. On the same site, or very nearby, had stood the playhouse (casino) of the Orsini family. The title, affixed after the writing, alluded to the fact that I was giving a gift from the studio to my friends in the Villa (or the Casino).

Straccio Vecchio. An old rag. Also one of the common cries at the great flea market in Rome, the *Porta Portese*. The shoddy material that comprises this piece fell off some fabric I was fashioning for *Trapunto Junction*, the Boston Symphony commission. Robert Levin, who loves sleazy modulations, seemed to be in mind as I stitched and darned; so I dedicated the piece to him.

The following three pieces all derive form from cells developed in *Trapunto Junction*. *Delirium Breve* is self explanatory. *From the Flow* sounds like a poetic and respectable title. It is not. *Addio, Addio Roma* is heartfelt and suggests regret. Leaving Rome was not easy. The actual words are sung by Ottavia, the heartbroken empress— "Regina Disprezzata"—as she faces exile from her beloved city in *L'Incoronazione di Poppea* by Claudio Monteverdi.

Post Fantasies

Sixty Points of Light was composed for Michael Putnam, Professor of Classics at Brown University, as a greeting on the occasion of his sixtieth birthday. I imagined the archangel Michael dispatching sixty of his legions to fight the devil.

L'Auberge de l'Ill began as a song evoking the memory of an exquisite restaurant in Alsace. The song was conceived as part of a song cycle entitled *Restaurants, Wines, Bistros, Shrines,* celebrating outstanding dining experiences shared with friends in France and Italy. While the words *"L'Auberge de l'Ill"* suggested the music for the beginning of the song, the music rapidly developed on its own, leaving the text far behind, and I found myself unable to invent a convincing continuation to the text. So, alternatively, the song became a piano piece, aspiring to become a song.

Three-fingered Don (also *Tree-fingered Don,* due to a typographical slip) was my contribution to a "Festschrift" in honor of Don Martino on his retirement, in 1993, from Harvard. The letters of his name determine the pitches upon which the composition is built. The title refers to Martino's Tin Pan Alley days in the middle 1950s when he was peddling his songs to the "pop" moguls on Broadway. He'd sing the lyrics and play the piano with two fingers of one hand and one of the other.

Sauce 180. Music 180 is the exalted chamber music class at Harvard, whose eminent alumni include Yo-Yo Ma, Lynn Chang, James Buswell, Max Levinson, and Christopher Taylor. For the past nine years the class has been guided by Robert Levin (with Daniel Stepner) and to celebrate the conclusion of a successful fall semester in 1994, Levin was giving a party for all participants. He proposed a "pasta party" with a homemade sauce, rich with "fragrance and unctiousness." The key words stuck in my mind and I wrote this fragrant and unctious little song to the text, "fragrance and unctiousness." The piano piece is the song without the extreme unction of the text.

P.S. Although invited, I was unable to attend the party so I can give no opinion about the sauce.

The composition of *Mano a Mano* was precipitated by a frightening incident. My friend Robert Levin took a fall and injured a hand, and the immediate prognosis was unclear. He made a rapid recovery, however, and was able to resume his performance wizardry in a short time. *Mano a Mano* in its original form was preceded by a short recitative - *Mano Caduta* (fallen hand) - alluding to the accident. The "text" goes:

> Bobby's injury is minor
> and it could have been much worse.
> It could have been major,
> a manual apocalypse!
> With abuse it could augment;
> with care it could diminish,
> not dominate his life!
> > And now we shall see
> > the signs of true recovery.
> > Can you play this?
> > It's the true test…

The Hanover Ketubah was written as wedding present for friends who were in residence at Dartmouth College.

Yehudi Wyner

FANTASIES FOR PIANO
THREE SHORT FANTASIES

Yehudi Wyner

for Pat and Bud
Short Fantasy 1

2

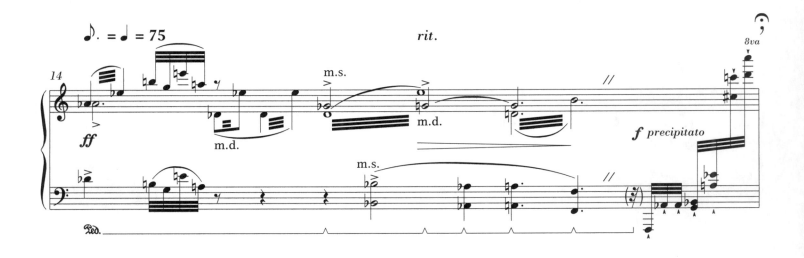

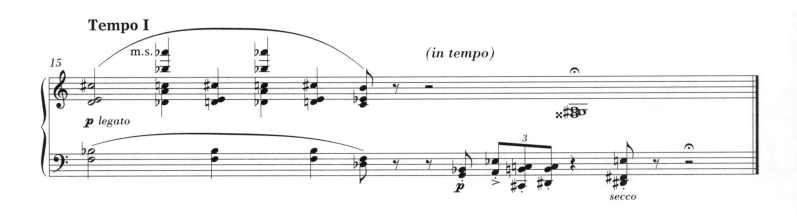

Short Fantasy 2
(Piccola Fantasia Davenniana)

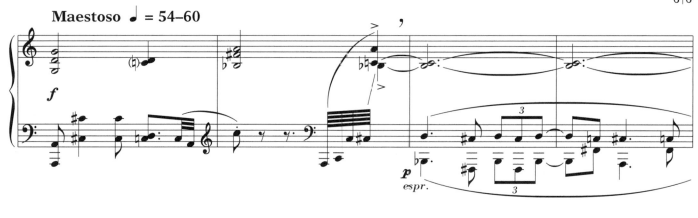

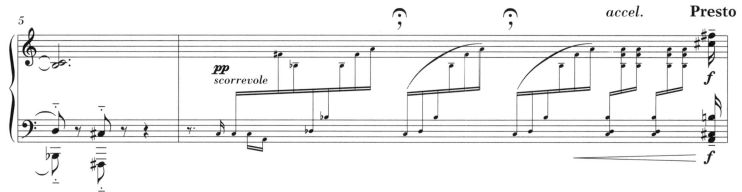

Più presto ♩ = 160

* Grace notes immediately follow chord.

Affectionately composed for Ward Davenny on his 50th birthday

for Robert Miller
Short Fantasy 3

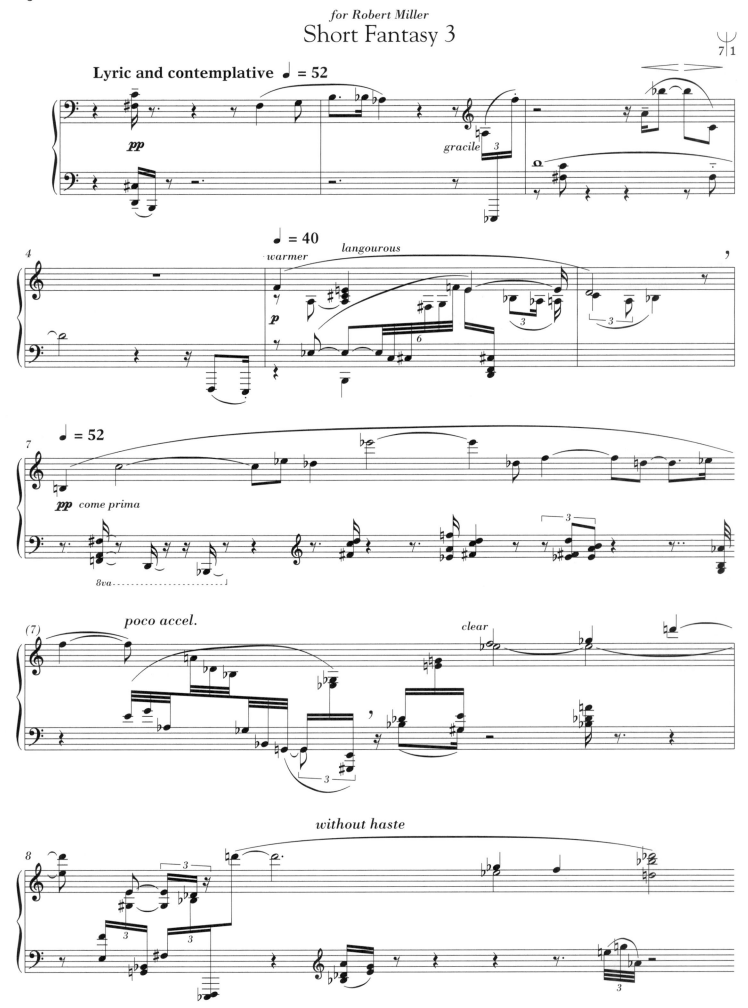

NEW FANTASIES

for Michael and Ken

Dalla Cappella al Casino

Yehudi Wyner

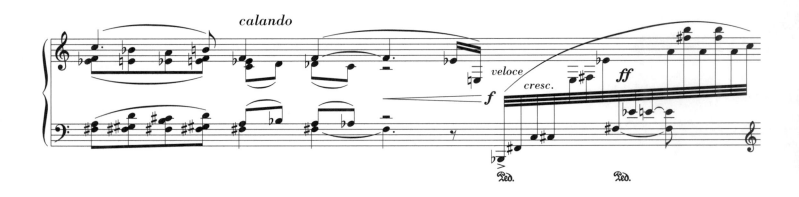

Tempo I

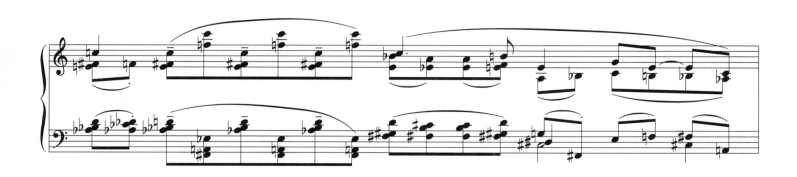

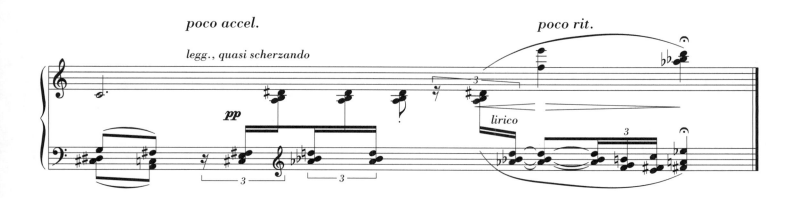

for Robert Levin
Stracchio Vecchio

for Dorothea Rockburne
Delirium Breve

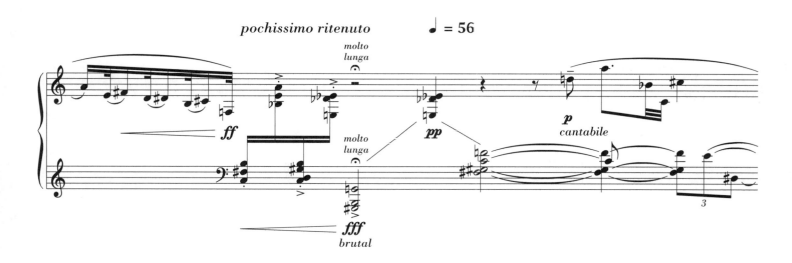

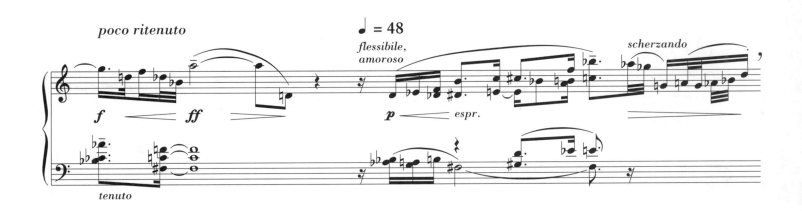

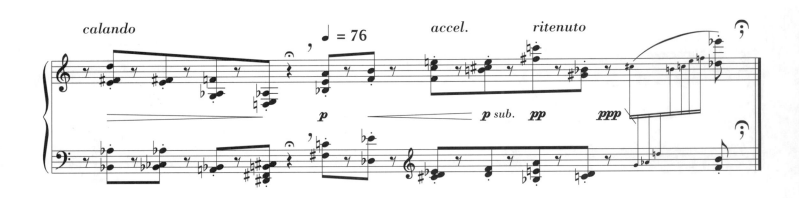

for Steve Malawista
From the Flow

Quicker at once

♩ = 172

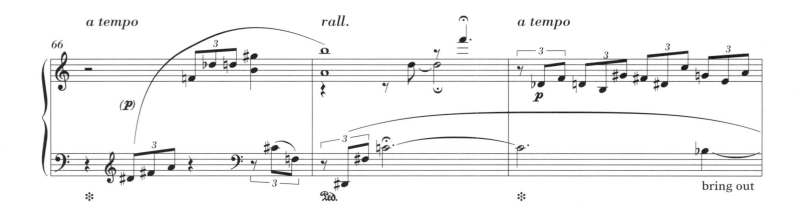

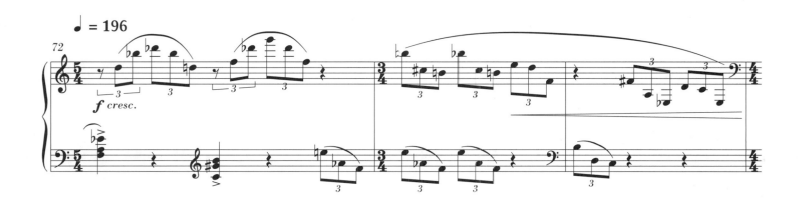

Tempo I, manic ♩ = 150

animato

leggiero

Senza misura, presto possibile

8va

lunga

blurring

Addio, Addio Roma

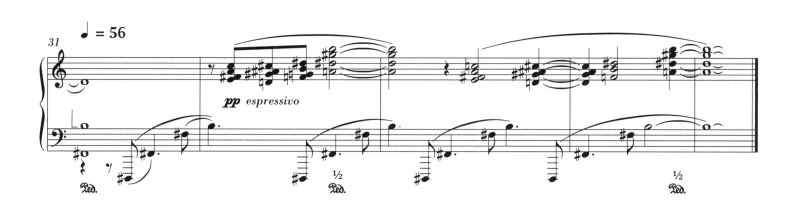

POST FANTASIES

for Michael Putnam

Sixty Points of Light

Yehudi Wyner

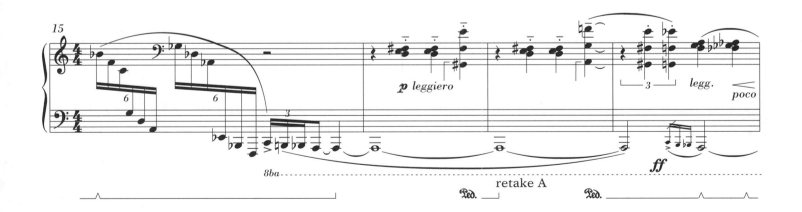

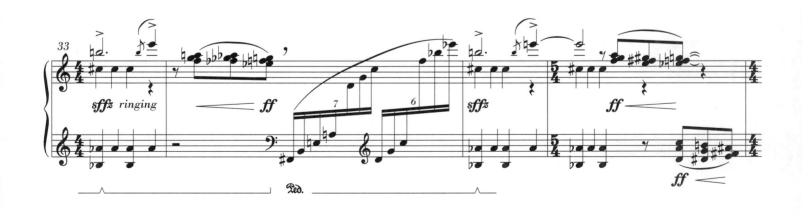

for Tobé Malawista
L'Auberge de l'Ill

from *Restaurants, Wines, Bistros, Shrines*

Subdued and expressive ♩ = 54

Three-fingered Don

Slummy ♩ = 152
Swing feel, ♫ ≅ ♪♪

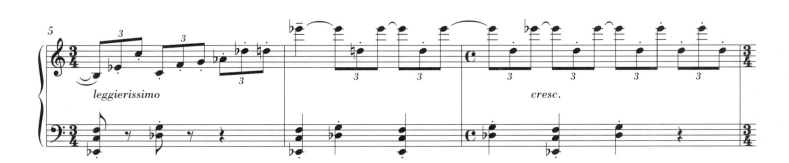

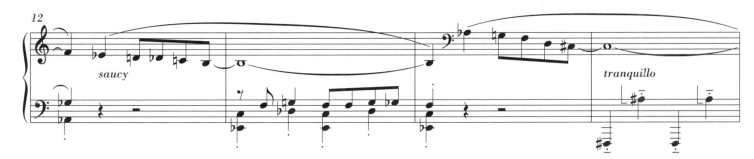

Sauce 180

for Robert Levin
Mano a Mano

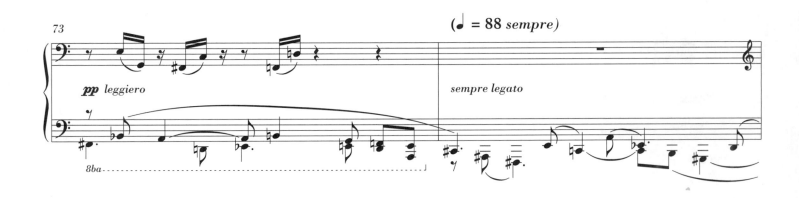

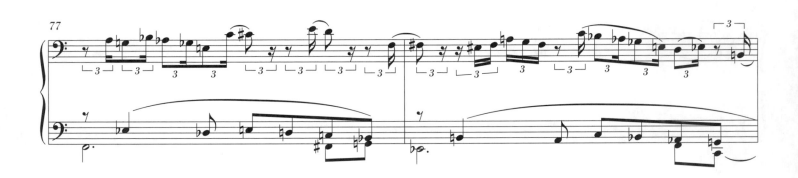

for Mary and Phil
The Hanover Ketubah

Gently flexible ♩ = ca. 54